21st
Century
Skills Library

COOL STEM CAREERS

INFORMATION SECURITY ANALYST

WIL MARA

Published in the United States of America by
Cherry Lake Publishing, Ann Arbor, Michigan
www.cherrylakepublishing.com

Content Adviser
Charles Bartocci, PhD, Professor, Dabney S. Lancaster Community College, Clifton
Forge, Virginia

Photo Credits: Cover and page 1, ©Yang Liu/Media Bakery; page 4, ©Monkey
Business Images/Shutterstock, Inc.; page 6, ©Subbotina Anna/Shutterstock, Inc;
pages 11, 15, and 23, ©.shock/Shutterstock, Inc.; page 12, ©Geanina Bechea/
Shutterstock, Inc.; page 16, ©Eimantas Buzas/Shutterstock, Inc.; page 18,
©StockLite/Shutterstock, Inc.; page 20, ©Konstantin Chagin/Shutterstock, Inc.;
page 24, ©Zurijeta/Shutterstock, Inc.; page 26, ©Anna Lurye/Shutterstock, Inc.;
page 27, ©EDHAR/Shutterstock, Inc.

**Cataloging-in-Publication data is available from the Library of
Congress.**
978-1-62431-005-8 (lib. bdg.)
978-1-62431-029-4 (pbk.)
978-1-62431-053-9 (e-book)

Cherry Lake Publishing would like to acknowledge
the work of The Partnership for 21st Century Skills.
Please visit *www.21stcenturyskills.org* for more information.

Printed in the United States of America
Corporate Graphics Inc.
January 2013
CLSP12

TABLE OF CONTENTS

INFORMATION SECURITY ANALYST

CHAPTER ONE
DO YOU WANT TO KNOW A SECRET?

Eric is sitting in his office. Computer monitors are all around him. But only one has his attention this morning. He's been watching it a lot over the last few weeks.

Information security analysts keep a close eye on Internet use at their companies.

The company Eric works for is worth billions of dollars. It has dozens of divisions, thousands of products, and offices all over the world. Eric works at the company's main headquarters. This means the most powerful people in the company work in the same building as he does.

Eric's boss has been very nervous lately. She believes that someone inside the company has been stealing secrets about a new product they've been developing. The product could earn the company billions of dollars in profit. Those billions will be lost if she's right. She's been pushing Eric to find out if her suspicions are true. Eric has told her to be patient. But her patience is starting to run out. He keeps his eyes trained on that one monitor, waiting and hoping.

And then it suddenly happens. An identification code pops up on the screen. The code is a sequence of numbers separated by a few periods here and there. Eric knows exactly what it means. He picks up the phone and calls his boss. Then he places another call. After that, he bolts out of his office and hurries down the hallway. Two burly men in suits join him when he reaches the corner. There are other people around. They are unsure of what's going on. They step aside as the three men rush past.

Eric's boss seems to appear out of nowhere and trails close behind. At the end of the hall, Eric and the two men reach the door to one of the bathrooms. They burst in. It doesn't seem as though anyone's in there. Eric knows better. "Over there," he says. "It's the one at the end." The two men go to the last stall and push open the door. Sure enough, an employee is typing furiously on an iPad. His face reddens and his shoulders sag when he looks up. He knows he's been caught.

Skilled computer users can break into computer networks and steal valuable information.

As the culprit is led out of the bathroom, Eric's boss tells the man that he will need a good lawyer. One of the company's top executives comes down an hour later to personally thank Eric for a job well done.

■ ■ ■

Does this story sound like something out of a suspense movie? It's not. The everyday responsibilities of being an information security analyst include tracking down people who violate **security policies**. The main goal of the information security business is preventing important information from falling into the wrong hands.

The desire to protect valuable information is nothing new. Examples of secret codes written by craftspeople to protect trade secrets have been found among ruins from the ancient civilization of Mesopotamia. This means that information security existed more than 7,000 years ago. Ancient Greek and Roman military leaders are believed to have used **ciphers**. Ciphers are methods of secret writing that can be understood only by the person receiving the message. Secret codes were also widely used during World Wars I and II. They were often used with the aid of **cryptographic** machines. These devices scrambled messages that were sent over telephone or telegraph wires so enemy forces could not intercept and decode them.

During World War II, American forces successfully used code breakers called Navajo code talkers. These were young Navajo Indian men who transmitted secret messages on battlefields in the Pacific Ocean region. The Navajo men devised a code that used native terms in place of military language. They also used native terms to represent the letters in the alphabet. To this day, it is the only unbroken code in modern military history.

Information security has taken on a whole new meaning in the computer age. The basics are the same, but the methods

LEARNING & INNOVATION SKILLS

During World War II, the German military sent thousands of **sensitive** messages with the aid of a scrambler called the Enigma machine. The Allied forces fighting the Germans eventually figured out how to decode these messages. As a result, they often knew what German forces were going to do ahead of time. Dwight Eisenhower, the supreme commander of the Allied forces and later the 34th president of the United States, said that cracking the Enigma code played a huge role in winning the war.

and technologies are more advanced than ever. This is good news for the people charged with protection duties. But remember that the bad guys also have access to most of the same technology. This means the good guys have to stay one step ahead of them!

No matter how much protection is built around sensitive information, sooner or later someone seems to figure out a way to get through it. Sensitive information is critical to many different organizations. Governments, corporations, schools, banks, and hospitals all need to protect information. Even everyday people in their homes have sensitive information to protect. For example, no one would want strangers getting into their financial records. Private information is important to everyone. This is why information security analysts are so important.

Above all, an information security analyst's job is to protect the sensitive information kept by an employer. Sometimes that means reviewing all current security policies to see if there are any flaws in the system. Analysts have to keep up on all the latest developments in the field. They pay attention to both what the bad guys are doing and what the good guys are doing.

An analyst may also have to spend time training the company's employees so they gain a better understanding of security and what can be done to support it. There will be times when the analyst will have to perform certain tasks in secret. This might sound like cool stuff, but it's very serious work. One security leak can change the lives of thousands of people. This means that being an information security analyst can be a very challenging career.

Do you think you can handle it?

Information security analysts are responsible for protecting their employers' most sensitive information.

CHAPTER TWO
GETTING THE JOB

There are very few colleges that offer specific degrees in information security analysis. Instead, people interested

Large companies operate massive computer networks where information is being transferred at almost all times.

in becoming analysts need to study a variety of subjects at whatever college or vocational/technical school they attend.

One of the basic requirements to land a job as an information security analyst is to have a detailed knowledge of computers. Incredible strides have been made in computer technology over the last few decades. Even the average home system is amazingly complex and powerful. A computer enables ordinary users to perform extraordinary functions. An information security analyst has to develop a deep familiarity with computer **software** and **hardware**. Both will play a role in an analyst's work.

An analyst needs to understand that just about all computer programs present potential security challenges. For example, an employee might be working on a sensitive document in a word processor. There are programs that could enable a **hacker** to watch what that person is doing from another computer. On a **Web browser**, employees could easily download a virus without even realizing it. The virus might record or copy critical information and send it back to the hacker. The analyst needs to keep up on all the latest threats and ensure that the company's security programs have the latest updates to defend against them.

Data encryption is a crucial part of any organization's security system. An analyst needs to know both the latest encryption standards and how to assure that the employer is using them. An analyst must know how to use security-monitoring programs. These keep an eye on the Internet, in-house networks, **virtual private networks**, and all transactions that go in and out of a company.

An information security analyst also has to stay on top of all hardware developments. Laptops, **mainframes**, and

21ST CENTURY CONTENT

By their very nature, networks present serious security challenges simply because the job of a network is to share information among computers. The analyst has to understand where the potential security holes are and how to strike a perfect balance between what information gets shared and what doesn't. Wireless networks are particularly open to security problems from outside a company because people using portable wireless devices can hack into them. People driving by in cars have violated some wireless networks. The hackers stop, download the information they need, and then quickly drive off.

Information security analysts need to rapidly identify and patch security holes.

everything from motherboards and processors to hard drives and **routers** present security issues.

Many of the subjects that relate to the information security field are taught in college or at technical and vocational schools. Computer science is the most obvious one. Another is telecommunications. Telecommunications can include anything from e-mail and texting to phone calls and faxing. Any process that involves one person communicating

Analysts work with both hardware and software.

information to another is of concern to a security analyst. Network and system administration skills are also critical. All of these subjects are taught in most colleges and will make you a more attractive candidate for an analyst's job. Not all security analyst positions require a bachelor's degree, but having one helps.

There are certain personality traits that will help in a security analyst career. Perhaps the most important is trustworthiness. Companies look for this above all else because an analyst will have access to an organization's most sensitive information. A good analyst needs excellent communication skills, too. The job requires being in frequent contact with everyone from entry-level workers to top executives. Being an excellent critical thinker and problem solver is also crucial. An analyst will often have to gather data concerning a problem, identify which bits of information are the most important, and then come up with effective solutions.

Security issues can cause a lot of anxiety within an organization. Part of the analyst's job is to provide a much-needed cool head. Patience is also a virtue, because security problems can be quite complicated. Sometimes easy answers or quick fixes are simply impossible. The analyst must be able to deal with these situations and invest the time necessary to come up with the right solutions.

CHAPTER THREE
A DAY IN THE LIFE

An information security analyst usually performs a variety of tasks during the course of a day. This usually means the day is quite busy. But the various challenges bring excitement and stimulation to the job.

Security analysts sometimes spend time showing other employees how to avoid putting the company's network at risk.

One common responsibility is the routine monitoring of the employer's security system. This doesn't necessarily require an analyst to sit at a desk and stare at computer screens every moment of every hour. But regular checks have to be performed. The analyst has to respond to problems quickly when they arise.

The average monitoring system will likely report almost any activity that looks suspicious. The security analyst then has to determine which threats are serious and which are not. Even the best monitoring systems cannot make this judgment every time. This is why the human element is so important. Many security analysts have portable wireless devices to alert them of potential problems. If a security analyst is away from the office, an alert can be transferred to his or her cell phone.

Another critical daily task is to review security problems that have already been identified and then decide on a course of action. Sometimes an employee causes a security **breach** by accident. The analyst may be required to teach that person how to avoid making the same mistake in the future. If an employee violates a security policy on purpose, the analyst will most likely have to report the incident to a higher authority.

Once a serious security breach has occurred, the analyst is responsible for determining the best way to patch the hole in the system. A more permanent defense will be put in place later. The analyst is required to document each incident and provide detailed reports to the employer.

An analyst spends a fair amount of time evaluating and updating the employer's security system. A good analyst knows that a breach can occur at any moment. Talented hackers are always probing a system in search of a weakness.

No security system is 100 percent foolproof, but an analyst can fend off potential attacks by constantly reviewing

Information security analysts sometimes work together to solve difficult problems.

the system. This sometimes requires the analyst to run tests. An analyst may have to design tests that push the system to its limits. Similarly, an analyst has to test the system each time major updates are applied or when new software or hardware is installed. When a new operating system is put in place, for example, security problems are sure to occur. During these times, an information security analyst must do the very best.

An analyst may be required to provide security training to other employees. An analyst who reaches a high enough position within an organization may end up being in charge of a team. The analyst will have to teach his team members certain aspects of how the system works. This can be tricky. The analyst must pick people who are trustworthy and then decide how much information they really need to know.

Analysts may have to train workers who are not under their direct supervision. This may involve giving classes on what to do if a security violation has taken place and what the consequences could be if someone breaches the system on purpose.

Sometimes an information security analyst may be asked to design a system from the ground up. This might happen when a new company has been launched or when an existing organization is looking to improve or replace its equipment. The analyst will design complex systems, draw up plans, and write reports and recommendations. Sometimes a company will hire an outside analyst to do this work. This analyst will probably be asked to remain on hand while the system is put in place. Any bugs that show up in the system once it's up and running will have to be ironed out. The analyst will run test after test, and continually refine the system to assure that any problems are found and fixed long before it goes live.

LEARNING & INNOVATION SKILLS

There are times when an organization needs to move data from one place to another. In many cases, simple encryption will be sufficient. Other times, an analyst may have to get creative. Before the final Harry Potter book was published, an electronic version of it was moved from one place to another in an interesting fashion. The person chosen to carry the digital file of the book kept it on a portable USB drive. That way, the file was not moved over the Internet. Only a handful of people knew he was carrying the file from one location to another. If the USB drive fell into the wrong hands, the company could have erased its contents remotely, via satellite. This complex plan of protection is the kind of work an information security analyst might be called upon to do.

Analysts think creatively to outwit hackers who might try to steal information.

CHAPTER FOUR
LOOKING AHEAD

The future looks bright for information security analysts. First, most of these jobs are tied directly to computer

Companies and government organizations will continue to need information security analysts in the future.

technology, and computers are obviously here to stay. Virtually all organizations use them, so there will certainly be a need for data protection. Additionally, there will always be dishonest people trying to get their hands on information they shouldn't have. If everyone were honest, there'd be no need for security systems in the first place!

Most experts believe that the need for information security analysts will continue to grow in the years ahead. In 2010, there were slightly more than 300,000 analyst jobs in the United States. Some experts estimate that by 2020, the number of analyst jobs will be about 370,000, or about 22 percent more.

Information security analysts in the United States earn about $75,000 per year. Exact amounts depend on work experience, location, and demand. Most employers are looking for people with at least two to three years of experience. A bachelor's degree can also help land a job. Health benefits are almost always included in the employment package because analysts are usually hired by large organizations. Also included in the package will be sick time, vacation time, personal time, a retirement plan, and possibly even a life insurance plan.

Do you enjoy working with computers? Do you have both an analytical and a creative side? Then you might want to consider becoming an information security analyst. As an information security analyst, you will be able to take pride in knowing that your employer relies on you to protect the company's most precious secrets. Technology will continue to develop. Dishonest people will become better at breaking

Information security jobs can be stressful, but they can be rewarding for people who enjoy working with computers.

Do you have what it takes to fend off hackers and keep information safe?

down cyberdefenses. This means the job of information security analysts will become more challenging in years to come. For many people, this will make the job even more rewarding.

 ## LIFE & CAREER SKILLS

Most of the skills and training that help a person become an information security analyst are useful in a wide variety of other professions. An incident responder, for example, specializes in hands-on response to security breaches, including closing holes in a security system and tracking down violators. A forensic analyst searches for answers once a cybercrime has been committed. A computer crime investigator's job is to determine how a breach was committed, what tools were used, and—perhaps most importantly—who made the breach.

SOME WELL-KNOWN INFORMATION SECURITY ANALYSTS

Ross Anderson (1956–) is a British-born researcher and consultant in information security and a professor in security engineering at the University of Cambridge in England. He has designed several notable cryptographic programs that are used to build computer security systems.

Eli Biham is an Israeli cryptographer and professor in the computer science department at the Technion Israeli Institute of Technology in Haifa, Israel. He has designed numerous cryptographic programs for computer security systems and has worked with British researcher Ross Anderson, Australian cryptographer Jennifer Seberry, and Danish researcher Lars Knudsen.

Julius Caesar (100 BCE–44 BCE) was a Roman dictator and military leader. He invented the Caesar cipher to prevent his secret messages from being read if they fell into enemy hands. In the system, each letter in the alphabet is replaced by another letter a fixed number of positions down the alphabet. For example, using a shift of four, A would be replaced by E, B would be replaced by F, and so on.

GLOSSARY

breach (BREECH) a violation

ciphers (SYE-furz) systems of writing in which characters are changed or substituted for other characters

cryptographic (krip-tuh-GRAF-ik) referring to a system or device using a secret code to write and decode messages

data encryption (DAY-tuh en-KRIP-shun) the ability to disguise important data so it can be read only by the person or people who are supposed to have it

hacker (HAK-ur) someone who gets into a computer system without permission

hardware (HAHRD-wair) computer equipment, such as a printer, monitor, or keyboard

mainframes (MAYN-fraimz) large, powerful computers that can help run smaller computers

routers (RAUT-urz) devices that handle signals between computers or computer networks

security policies (si-KYOOR-uh-tee PAHL-uh-seez) rules and regulations that govern a system of computers

sensitive (SEN-suh-tiv) requiring careful handling

software (SAWFT-wair) computer programs that control the workings of the hardware and direct it to do special tasks

virtual private networks (VUR-choo-uhl PRYE-vut NET-wurks) secure connections to an internal network through an outside computer

Web browser (WEB BROUZ-ur) a computer program that lets you find and look through Web pages or other data

FOR MORE INFORMATION

BOOKS

Covaleski, John. *Hacking*. San Diego, CA: ReferencePoint Press, 2013.

Harmon, Daniel E. *Careers in Internet Security*. New York: Rosen Publishing, 2011.

Hubbard, Ben. *Code Breakers*. New York: Crabtree Publishing, 2010.

Levete, Sarah. *Taking Action Against Internet Crime*. New York: Rosen Central, 2010.

Mooney, Carla. *Online Security*. San Diego, CA: ReferencePoint Press, 2012.

WEB SITES

InfoSecurity: Educating Children on Data Protection
www.infosecurity-magazine.com/view/848/educating-children-on-data-protection
Learn what threats to watch for on your home or school computer, what you can do to minimize the chances of a cyberattack, and more.

SafeKids.com
www.safekids.com
Check out tips and advice that cover topics from online searches to social networking etiquette.

21ST CENTURY SKILLS LIBRARY

INDEX

ABOUT THE AUTHOR

Wil Mara is the award-winning author of more than 130 books, many of which are educational titles for young readers. Further information about his work can be found at www.wilmara.com.